Sequoyah: The Life and Legacy of the Most Famous Cherokee

By Dr. Jesse Harasta and Charles River Editors

Picture of the statue of Sequoyah in the U.S. Capitol

About Charles River Editors

Charles River Editors provides superior editing and original writing services across the digital publishing industry, with the expertise to create digital content for publishers across a vast range of subject matter. In addition to providing original digital content for third party publishers, we also republish civilization's greatest literary works, bringing them to new generations of readers via ebooks.

Sign up here to receive updates about free books as we publish them, and visit Our Kindle Author Page to browse today's free promotions and our most recently published Kindle titles.

Introduction

Sequoyah (circa 1770s-1840s)

Tragically, the Cherokee is one of America's best known tribes due to the trials and tribulations they suffered by being forcibly moved west along the "Trail of Tears", but that overlooks the contributions they made to American society well before the 19th century. The Cherokee began the process of assimilation into European America very early, even before the establishment of the Unites States, and by the early 19th century they were one of the "Five Civilized Tribes." Despite all of the hostilities and the Trail of Tears, the Cherokee ultimately became the first people of non-European descent to become U.S. citizens en masse, and today the Cherokee Nation is the largest federally recognized tribe in the United States, boasting over 300,000 members.

The Cherokee might be the most famous tribe in the country, and if so, the person most responsible for it is Sequoyah, whose invention of the Cherokee syllabary also played a prominent role in facilitating the assimilation between the Cherokee and Americans. Sequoyah began work on devising the writing and reading system around 1809, and it was instantly popular among the Cherokee, to the extent that it was being used in written publications among the tribe by the 1820s. The syllabary has been in use ever since, both within the tribe and among outsiders.

Thanks to his accomplishments, Sequoyah was celebrated in his own lifetime, but due to his obscure roots, accounts of his early years still vary dramatically. *Sequoyah: The Life and Legacy of the Most Famous Cherokee* looks at the life and work of the man who put the Cherokee language down in print and made it possible for outsiders to both read and write it. This includes analyzing the nature of his invention, the social context in which he lived, and the ongoing legacy he has left for the modern Cherokee. Along with pictures of important people, places, and events, you will learn about Sequoyah like never before, in no time at all.

Sequoyah: The Life and Legacy of the Most Famous Cherokee

About Charles River Editors

Introduction

Chapter 1: Cherokee History Before Sequoyah

Chapter 2: Who was Sequoyah?

Chapter 3: Adulthood and the Creation of the Syllabary

Chapter 4: Promotion of the Syllabary and the End of Sequoyah's Life

Chapter 5: Sequoyah's Syllabary and the "New Cherokee"

Chapter 6: Understanding the Syllabary

Chapter 7: The Cherokee Language

Chapter 8: Sequoyah's Modern Legacy

Bibliography

Chapter 1: Cherokee History Before Sequoyah

Like many Native American tribes, the Cherokee experienced "forced migrations," both at the hands of their fellow indigenous people and most infamously, during the Trail of Tears episode when they were forced from their homeland by the U.S. military. As a result, the Cherokee are often associated with the Deep South, but originally, the Cherokee lived in the northeastern part of the present-day United States, around the Great Lakes. At some time in the distant past, the tribe was forced out of the region, probably at the hands of a militarily stronger tribe. While it has long been believed that it was the Iroquois who forced the Cherokee to migrate south and settle in the present-day southeastern United States. Delaware tribal legends support the defeat of the Cherokee but Iroquois legends make no mention of such a story.

Today it is believed that the Cherokee migrated south thousands of years ago. The Cherokee language is part of the Iroquoian language family but has changed significantly, indicating that the tribe left its ancestral homeland at least several millennia ago. Glottochronology is an anthropological technique of tracking linguistic changes in related languages to determine how long people groups sharing the root language have been separated. The technique studies core words and attempts to decipher the length of time needed to achieve perceived changes. Using this technique, researchers have estimated that the Cherokee departed from the Iroquois ancestors about 6,000 years ago. However, because language does not leave archaeological evidence, this estimate is far from certain.

The name Cherokee is likely derived from the Creek word chelokee, which means "people of a different speech." Also, though many Cherokee people accept the term "Cherokee," some prefer and use the word "Tsalagi" to refer to themselves and their tribe. Originally, the Cherokee referred to themselves as the Aniyunwiya or Anniyaya which can be translated as "the principal people. This moniker understandably fits with the Cherokee creation narrative, in which the Cherokee are the first (among many) Native American tribes to occupy the Earth. They also called themselves the Keetoowah, meaning the "people of Kituhwa." Other indigenous tribes had names for the Cherokee, many of which resemble Cherokee, Tsalagi, and Keetoohwa. A few examples are: Chilukki (used by the Choctaw and Chickasaw and meaning "dog people"), Talligewi (used by the Delaware people), and Kittuwa (used by the Algonquin people).

From their northeastern origins, the Cherokee migrated to the present-day southeastern United States to settle in a region currently composed of parts of western North and South Carolina, Northern Georgia, southwestern Virginia, and the Cumberland Basin of Tennessee, Kentucky, and northern Alabama. While the tribe's population prior to European contact remains unknown, it is estimated that epidemics beginning in 1540 (the date of first contact with the DeSoto Expedition) likely killed at least 75% of the tribe's population. By 1674, the Cherokee had rebounded to about 50,000 members, but a series of epidemics in 1729, 1738, and 1753 further reduced this number by half. Just prior to their removal in the late 1830s, the population was around 25,000 and relatively stable.

The Cherokee tribe has traditionally been divided into three sub-groups based upon location and the distinct dialect of the Cherokee language. The Lower Cherokee lived in the eastern-most villages, and the Over-the-Hill Cherokee were those who occupied the western-most towns. As their designation implies, the Middle Cherokee occupied the territory between the two aforementioned groups. In addition to these three groups, several other distinctive bands of Cherokee people are identified as the Chickamauga, Onnontiogg, and Qualia. Also identified are two bands – the Atali and the Etali – whose names suggest that they may be one band that was given two different names by those who recorded them.

The first contact with Cherokee people made by Europeans occurred in 1540, when members of the de Soto Expedition recorded that they had found "Chalaque" settlements along the Tennessee River. The Spanish established and maintained a small mining and smelting operation that remained in the region until around 1690, but because the Cherokee generally lived in remote mountainous regions, they were able to avoid frequent contact with European settlers until about 1609, when the colony of Virginia was established.

By 1629, English settlers had entered the Appalachian Mountains and came into contact with Cherokee villages, and after the founding of the Carolina colonies, European contact with the Cherokee became almost constant. An expedition sent by Virginia-based trader Abraham Wood established a trading network with Cherokee living in their capital at Echota in present-day northern Alabama in 1673. Though Virginia traders attempted to maintain a monopoly on the lucrative trade in animal skins and Native American slaves with the Cherokee, the enterprising indigenous group approached newcomers from the Carolinas and established trade connections with them the following year as well. Traders from South Carolina established a treaty with Cherokee living in their area by 1684, and a steady flow of deerskins and slaves began to flow out of the Cherokee villages.

During this time, life among the Cherokee inevitably began to change as well. As contact with colonial traders increased, the level of dependence on European goods increased among the Cherokee. Moreover, the political power base within the Cherokee settlements shifted from the priest/shaman class to that of the hunter/warrior as the latter became "hunters for profit." The increasing reliance on European goods from the English colonies also caused the Cherokee to ally themselves with the English against the Spanish and French during conflicts between 1689 and 1763. This was a natural byproduct of the fact that Cherokee warriors raided Spanish settlements in present-day northern Florida in the 1670s, and they were also fighting with the coastal tribes in the Carolinas.

The frequent warring between the Native American tribes was exacerbated by the fact that the Europeans introduced superior military technology to them upon their arrival. By 1680, most tribes in the region had acquired firearms, forcing the larger Cherokee settlements throughout the region to become more militarized and fortified against attack. Also during this period, conflicts with the Catawba to the east and the Choctaw and Creek to the south escalated until the tribes were engaged in almost constant fighting. Traditional enmity with the Chickasaw, another Native American tribe allied with the British, also kept the Cherokee busy with fighting to the west. On top of all that, there were territory conflicts along the northern frontiers of Cherokee territory between English, French, and Dutch traders.

While the Cherokee fought their traditional enemies and the European conflict evolved into the Beaver Wars, the expanding and powerful Iroquois League pushed Native Americans out of the Great Lakes, creating a stream of refugees that headed south and also came into contact with the Cherokee. As a result, during the mid-17th century, large numbers of Shawnee people were forced out of their traditional homelands by powerful Iroquois bands, and these refugees entered traditionally Cherokee territory. Taking advantage of the situation and essentially using the Shawnee as a buffer, the Cherokee allowed the refugees to settle between themselves and their regional enemies. One Shawnee group was allowed to settle in South Carolina between Cherokee towns and the Catawba tribe, and a second group was allowed to settle in the Cumberland Basin of Tennessee as a buffer between the Cherokee and the Chickasaw.

This decision eventually proved problematic for the Cherokee when the Iroquois, remembering their enemies, ventured south and raided Shawnee and Cherokee settlements. Eventually, the Shawnee grew into a threat to the Cherokee as well, and in the late 17th century, Shawnee raiders destroyed a major Cherokee town while raiding it for slaves because the village's warriors were away on a hunt. The raid destroyed the fragile trust that had existed between the Cherokee and Shawnee, and the following year a group of Cherokee leaders traveled to Charlestown and asked for additional firearms to defend their villages against raiders bent on capturing slaves for the lucrative South Carolina trade.

Attitudes among the Cherokee in the Carolinas were so dangerously inflammatory that during the first decade of the 18th century, North Carolina officials demanded that South Carolina traders curtail the Native American slave trade for fear of a general rebellion. British government officials eventually stepped in and brokered a peace treaty between the Iroquois and the Cherokee, and over the course of the next 10 years, Cherokee warriors allied with different partners – both colonials and fellow Native American tribes – to secure their region and rid themselves of common enemies. Still, the Shawnee problem remained, and in 1715 Cherokee warriors entered into an alliance with their old adversaries, the Chickasaw. Together, the two tribes dealt a crippling blow to the Shawnee in the Cumberland Basin, but their alliance attracted the attention of both the French traders and their Algonquin allies, who began a series of raids against Cherokee villages from strongholds north of the Ohio River.

This period of conflict would last until the middle of the 18th century, during which time the Cherokee found themselves fighting Native American allies of both the British (the Iroquois) and the French (the Algonquins). Finally, in 1745, the Cherokee again allied with the Chickasaw and drove the remaining Shawnee over the Ohio River and out of Cherokee territory for good. The alliance then turned on another common enemy and French ally, the Choctaw, and defeated them in 1750.

The first half of the 18th century also saw the first land ceded to white settlers by the Cherokee. In a treaty between British colonists and Cherokee tribal members in 1721, a boundary between Cherokee and British settlements was established, but North Carolina and South Carolina settlers were soon making incursions into Lower Cherokee territory east of the Appalachians anyway. Additionally, French traders had established a trading post near Montgomery, Alabama in 1717 and made contact with the Over-the-Hill Cherokee by navigating along the Cumberland River. Many Cherokee were tempted to switch their allegiance from the British to the French, but practical realities dissuaded them. French goods were of lower quality than those provided by the British, and the British had the naval power to effectively cut off French colonies in Canada by blockading the northeast points of entry. Also, the Chickasaw made navigation on the Tennessee River, a major trading route, virtually impossible for the French.

The British, sensing that the Cherokee might be tempted by French offers of allegiance, sent representatives to regulate trade and streamline trade relations by urging the Cherokee to appoint a single chief for each town, and British influence also led to peace treaties between the Cherokee and their former enemies the Catawba and the Wyandot tribes. During these peace negotiations, the Cherokee learned that the Wyandot and other Native American tribes were secretly planning to abandon their trade alliances with the French, information that ended any further consideration of the French as a trade alternative to the British. In the end, the French were simply unable to compete with the British in terms of quality of goods and access to Native American trading partners.

At the same time, the British remained concerned that the Cherokee would switch alliances, and they weren't entirely concerned about maintaining their end of the land bargains they struck with the Cherokee. Throughout the remainder of the 18th century, the Cherokee lost land to British colonists invading and settling on their land, and the tribe alternated between fighting against them and for them.

During the American Revolution, the Cherokee sided with the British, and the decision cost them heavily. Cherokee war parties engaged in several unsuccessful raids against American settlements, and the colonists responded with several victories, forcing the Cherokee to sue for peace. In the ensuing peace negotiations, the Cherokee gave up their ancestral and historical claims to territory in North Carolina and South Carolina, codified in the Treaty of DeWitts Corner (1777) and the Treaties of Long Island of Holston drafted in 1777 and 1781. The defeats and the territorial concessions would induce the Cherokee to strive for assimilation into American society in the early 19th century, a crucial aspect to Sequoyah's life and his invention of the Cherokee syllabary.

Chapter 2: Who was Sequoyah?

Sculpted depiction of Sequoyah on the Library of Congress, John Adams Building

Like many Native Americans, Sequoyah had two names, one in his native tongue and one in English. His Cherokee language name, ⬜ ⬜⬜,, has been variously spelled in English as Sequoia, Ssiquoya or (most frequently) Sequoyah. Meanwhile, during his lifetime, in English he was known by the name given to him by whites, his father's people: George Gist or George Guess.

This diversity of names should not be surprising, in part thanks to the man himself. The

Sequoyah/Ssiquoya/Sequoia options are due to debates about how to capture the sounds of Sequoyah's own syllabary in the English alphabet, and similar debates occur whenever words in one writing system are transferred into another (such as in the case of Beijing/Peking/Peiping, all attempts to capture the sounds of Chinese in English). The fact that he also had an English name is only partly due to his mixed heritage; Native Americans being given European names was a common occurrence in a world where Christian missionaries and government agents sought to remove any trace of "Indian" culture from the native peoples, including names. The fact that his father's name may have been spelled "Gist" or "Guess" is due to the fact that spellings, even for last names, were not standardized until the era of modern governmental record-keeping. For example, William Shakespeare used numerous versions of his own last name, including "Shakespear," "Shakp," "Shakspēr," "Shakspere" and "Shakspeare." Sequoyah would have had the freedom to use "Gist" or "Guess" based upon his whims of the moment, and regardless of which last name he used, no one would have batted an eye.

Like many people in the colonial Southeast, Sequoyah was of mixed ancestry, and many of his neighbors also would have had some mixture of native, European and African ancestry. By the late 18th century, membership in the Native or Colonial society was less a matter of race (a still-amorphous quality in many border communities) and instead one of political and cultural allegiance[1]. Sequoyah's mother was Wuh-the, a member of the Cherokee nation who was born in the village of Tuskeegee (or sometimes spelled "Tuskigi"). Little is known about her today except for her lineage, as she was the daughter of one of the village's hereditary leaders. His father was Nathaniel Gist (Guess), a white fur trader from Virginia of southwest British ancestry. One oral tradition holds that Nathaniel Gist was an American patriot who traveled to Tuskeegee as an agent of the Revolutionary military trying to generate support among the Cherokee[2]. Today the Gist name is found primarily in South Carolina and Texas, but it was not uncommon for a fur trader in those days to range widely, so the name is scattered throughout the Southeast[3] (though not among the Cherokee themselves[4]).

The town of Tuskeegee was not the same as the modern town in Alabama (Tuskegee) but was instead located in today's Tennessee, which was still Cherokee territory at the time. Tuskeegee was located at the junction of the Little Tennessee and Tellico Rivers, and archaeological work has determined that this strategic spot had been occupied periodically since the earliest habitation of the region. However, Tuskeegee was a relatively recent settlement that had grown up alongside a British frontier fortification called Fort Loudoun, which was built in 1756 by the colonies of South Carolina and Virginia for use during the French and Indian War (part of the

---

1 *Red, White & Black: The People of Early North America* by Gary B. Nash (1992). Prentice Hall Books.
2 This may be true, but it also has the ring of historic revisionism in an attempt to make Sequoyah into a patriotic American with roots in the Revolution and therefore more palatable to White society.
3 "Gist Family History" at *Ancestry.com* accessed online at: http://www.ancestry.com/name-origin?surname=gist
4 Probably due to Sequoyah's own rejection of his English name. Numerous English-origin surnames have entered Native communities through similar paths, such as the Jamisons of the Seneca Nation who all trace their lineage to Mary Jamison, the so-called "White Woman of the Genessee" (1743-1833).

broader Seven Years War). The purpose of the fort had been twofold: to protect the Cherokee from devastating raids from French-allied groups further inland, and also to keep the Cherokee tied militarily and politically to the colony of South Carolina. Eventually, relations between the British and the Cherokee (who had assisted in the Fort's construction) soured, and the Cherokee successfully besieged and captured the Fort in 1760. This would precipitate an invasion of the region, known as the Overhill Country, by the British in 1761, but not the reconstruction of the Fort. However, Tuskeegee continued in the shadow of the ruins, existing until the 1790s, when the Cherokee surrendered the territory to the American government.

The Cherokee and the South Carolina colony were deeply interconnected throughout the early 1700s. For instance, in the 1740s, half of the entire colony's exports originated in trade with the Cherokee[5]. While this relationship would sour over time, with increasing suspicion and hostility on both sides, life in Tuskeegee in the 1770s was very much a product of this broad trading world. Archaeology in Tuskeegee has found that the Cherokee residents of Tuskeegee, far from stereotypes of savages (noble or otherwise) with stone arrows in the forest, had material lives very similar to their European neighbors, with household items made of fired crockery and colored glass, iron nails, brass objects, silver jewelry, rifles and metal tools. Undoubtedly, they also had woven cloth and elaborate personal decoration, which can be seen in images from the time of other Cherokee groups but did not preserve in the soils of Tuskeegee. Tuskeegee had a quarry where the residents cut limestone blocks, and in conjunction with timbers hewn from the forest, the inhabitants were able to construct sturdy rectangular homes[6].

Despite these similarities in technological sophistication, there were major cultural differences between Tuskeegee and white settlements of the time. A visitor would have first noticed the aural differences, as the people in Tuskeegee spoke the Cherokee language. Their styles of clothing and personal decoration varied greatly from European ones, and Cherokee homes were different as well, with separate summer and winter dwellings adapted to the local climate at the time. Despite the presence of an increasing number of Christian missionaries, there was also still a vibrant traditional religious life that would eventually lead to the creation of modern Cherokee religious groups like the Original Keetoowah Society and the Four Mothers Society. The community also had a traditional governmental structure, a system of local headmen that would eventually be absorbed into one of the three modern Cherokee tribal groups, in particular the Cherokee Nation. In all of these ways, none of which involved a greater or lesser level of "civilization" or technology, the Cherokee village of Sequoyah's youth was quite culturally

---

5   "Fort Loudoun in Tennessee: 1756-1760. History, Archaeology, Replication, Exhibits, and Interpretation" by Carl Kuttruff (2010). A report of the Tennessee Wars Commission and Tennessee Division of Archaeology. Research Series No. 17. Accessed online at: https://www.tn.gov/environment/docs/arch_rs17_fort_loudoun_2010.pdf. Pg 23

6   "Fort Loudoun in Tennessee: 1756-1760. History, Archaeology, Replication, Exhibits, and Interpretation" by Carl Kuttruff (2010). A report of the Tennessee Wars Commission and Tennessee Division of Archaeology. Research Series No. 17. Accessed online at: https://www.tn.gov/environment/docs/arch_rs17_fort_loudoun_2010.pdf.

distinct from the surrounding white settlements.

It is true that the Europeans stood at the forefront of scientific and technological pursuits in the 18th century, but little of this would have been evident on the South Carolina frontier. Benjamin Franklin and a handful of his correspondents and contemporaries excepted, the colonists were remarkably isolated from the intellectual and cultural currents of European society and demonstrated a marked conservatism in aesthetics, architecture, and technology on the frontier[7]. A traveler visiting Tuskeegee and then traveling to the nearest European settlement would have found few (if any) differences in technological sophistication. As a result, it was not European superiority in firepower that led to the eventual defeat of the Cherokee but the combination of disease and internecine strife amongst native groups. The Cherokee, like all Native American peoples, had not been exposed to animal-borne ("zootic") illnesses before the arrival of Europeans and were devastated by wave after wave of illnesses like smallpox, pneumonia, flu, measles, mumps, and scarlet fever. On top of this, European powers were able to manipulate pre-existing conflicts to their advantage; in the 1700s, it was largely not Europeans who killed Cherokee but instead the Creek people allied with the French. It was Creek raids that forced the Cherokee into ever-deeper dependency upon the British. This story of disease and inter-native conflict repeated itself over and over again across the Americas, and in those places that Europeans could not exploit divisions amongst Native peoples, they were rarely able to get a foothold even with the advantages of disease[8].

However, this picture was not clear to either Natives nor Europeans on the ground in the 1700s and 1800s, because it became clear only in hindsight through 20th century scholarship. Thus, for young Sequoyah, a bright boy growing up in this context, the only major difference between his mother's people and father's people was the Europeans' use of writing, an advantage that provided a satisfying enough explanation of the growth of British power and waning of Cherokee power during his youth. Writing was well known to the Cherokee as a concept, but they did not have writing themselves. They realized that the British Empire was administered through writing and that a king across the ocean could send his words to his most distant outpost (like Fort Laudon) without the need for intermediaries who might distort his commands. Moreover, the Christian religion was fundamentally based upon reading, and it was one of the strongest arguments that missionaries made for its superiority. To the Cherokee in Tuskeegee, it seemed writing was the only European technology that was widely spread across the colonies that the Cherokee could not access.

Although there were whites who interacted with the Cherokee in Tuskeegee, it appears that there was no-one in Tuskeegee who was able to teach the clever boy to read. The soldiers at the Fort were driven out about 15 years before he was born (roughly 1776), and for reasons that remain unclear, Sequoyah's father did not teach him the English alphabet. It's possible the elder

---

7   *In Small Things Forgotten: An Archaeology of Early American Life* by James Deetz (1996). Anchor Books.
8   *1491: New Revelations of the Americas Before Columbus* by Charles C. Mann (2006). Vintage Books.

Gist was illiterate himself, or he may very well have abandoned his Native American wife and son. While Sequoyah certainly saw written English - a number of the characters in his syllabary are directly modeled off of English letters - there is no evidence that he could read them, and there is no relationship between the sounds in English and Cherokee. For example, in Sequoyah's syllabary, "G" is for the syllable "nah" and "4" is for the syllable "se." The syllabary itself is proof that Sequoyah didn't even have the rudimentary ability to read the English alphabet; after all, if he could, he probably would have created a Cherokee alphabet, not a syllabary, which was a form of writing basically unknown to Europeans at the time.

Chapter 3: Adulthood and the Creation of the Syllabary

As he reached adulthood, Sequoyah followed the path of many other Cherokee by leaving his home territory, which was surrendered to whites, and settling in Cherokee territory in today's Arkansas. It was there that he married a Cherokee woman named Sally and eventually had four children with her, including a daughter named Ayoka. Sequoyah also pursued a trade as a silversmith and possibly as a blacksmith. As was the custom among prestigious Cherokee families, Sequoyah also married a second wife, named U-ti-yu, with whom he had three children. He apparently possessed an artistic side as well, because he was also known as an accomplished painter.

In 1812, when he was probably in his mid-30s, Sequoyah enlisted in the American army against the British in the War of 1812, and he then continued on in the military during the Creek War of 1813-1814, when the allied Americans and Cherokee crushed the remaining Creek forces. The Cherokee were once again on the side of Carolina colonists against the Creek, who were now allied with the former masters of Fort Loudoun. It is probable that it was a desire to fight against the Creek, not serve the Americans, that motivated Sequoyah, as he demonstrated an intense loyalty to the Cherokee people throughout his life and never served American interests for their own sake. Moreover, the fact that he would later serve as a representative of his people meant that they also were comfortable with his service in the war[9].

The experience of serving in Andrew Jackson's army on its march to Louisiana and the eventual Battle of New Orleans had a transformative effect upon Sequoyah. While he and fellow Cherokees were fighting with Americans, he could see the power of writing, from soldiers receiving orders from distant commanders to the coordination of a campaign with great precision across a continent. He also saw the more intimate effect of writing, as American soldiers received letters from home and kept in contact with their loved ones. He, on the other hand, could not let his wives and children know that he was alive, much less hear about their daily lives.

---

9 "Sequoyah (ca. 1770 - ca. 1840)" at the *New Georgia Encyclopedia* by Ted Wadley (2002). Accessed online at: http://www.georgiaencyclopedia.org/articles/history-archaeology/sequoyah-ca-1770-ca-1840

An illustration of Jackson at the Battle of New Orleans

The creation of a writing system is no easy task, even for those who are already literate in another language. It requires that a creator must be aware of all of the individual sounds in the language and be able to differentiate between similar sounds that speakers differentiate between without ever considering them (for instance, in English, the "P" and "B" sounds are remarkably close). A competent script creator needs to be aware of dialectical differences between speakers of different regions and determine how to create a single unified written form that takes into account all of the variations. Moreover, as one develops the characters, attention must be paid to the fact that they are easy to write, simple, and different enough from each other that there is little or no confusion. This is particularly challenging when one must create as many symbols as Sequoyah did, 85 in total.

What made Sequoyah's work amazing is that in his case, all of this had to be done in his head because the fact that he was illiterate meant he couldn't make written notes. Thus, Sequoyah must have had a tremendous ear for the spoken tongue, a prodigious memory, and a keen awareness of the nature of language and speech. Fortunately, Sequoyah had a number of advantages in this project. First, he had seen English script and was aware of the basics of how it operated, and perhaps just as importantly, he was not only fluent in Cherokee but also knew

English and potentially both French and Creek. Creek would have doubtless been very useful to him since it was part of the Muskogean language family, which was as distinct from Cherokee as Turkish is from English[10]. Even a passing familiarity with these other languages would have given Sequoyah an awareness of how sounds differed in various languages and what was distinct about the pronunciation of Cherokee. All of that said, the recognition of these slim advantages should not diminish from the fact that Sequoyah's script is a remarkable achievement with few parallels in human history.

It is possible that Sequoyah began his project as early as 1812, but it's hard to know an exact starting date since it obviously began as a mental exercise, not a written project, so there is no record of the event left for scholars to find. The only tantalizing clue to this early period was a series of petroglyphs carved into the wall of a Cherokee burial cave in southeastern Kentucky that appear to be dated to 1818; the symbols are definitely Sequoyah's, and since they do not form words based on the finished syllabary, the carvings may have been a form of practice. This place was considered to be a holy spot, and it was said that Sequoyah came here to think regularly[11]. Regardless of the authenticity of the Kentucky cave carvings, Sequoyah was definitely working on the syllabary throughout the 1810s and had produced a final product by 1821. What he produced was a system of 85 or 86 characters, depending on which version one reads.

Sequoyah also created a system of numerals with individual symbols for numbers 1 through 20, as well as distinct numbers for 30, 40, 50, 60, 70, 80, 90 and 100. While innovative, this system was never adopted by the Cherokee leadership, which instead decided to opt for the Arabic numerals. This is not surprising given that every society on Earth adopted the Arabic system for their ease of calculation and inter-language communication.[12]

Chapter 4: Promotion of the Syllabary and the End of Sequoyah's Life

Sequoyah's first student was his own young daughter, Ayoka. He created a game to teach her the symbols, and she picked them up quickly. This success encouraged Sequoyah to begin teaching his script to a wider audience, and between 1821 and 1825, he was engaged primarily in promoting the new writing system. In this, he had massive success, in part because the Cherokee were already widely familiar with English writing, and, like Sequoyah, many of them had firsthand experience with how effective written communications could be. However, written English was also strongly associated with institutions that the Cherokee had many reasons to be suspicious of, particularly Christian missionaries and the American and European governments and military.

---

10 "Muskogee" at the *Ethnologue* website. Accessed online at: http://www.ethnologue.com/language/mus
11 "Carvings from Cherokee Script's Dawn" by John Noble Wilford in the *New York Times* accessed online at: http://www.nytimes.com/2009/06/23/science/23cherokee.html?ref=science&_r=0
12 "Sequoyah's Numerals." Accessed online at: http://web.archive.org/web/20111102075444/http://intertribal.net/NAT/Cherokee/WebPgCC1/Numerals.htm

Sequoyah's system provided them with a unique path that provided all the benefits of writing without the drawbacks of utilizing a European system associated with the white settlers that were increasingly pushing them from their land. It was a win-win situation, and the Cherokee grasped its implications immediately, signing up to learn Sequoyah's system in droves. The uniqueness of the script also added to its appeal, as it was distinctly Cherokee and quickly became a matter of supreme pride amongst its users.

This pride in the distinctiveness (and, presumably, beauty) of one's script is overlooked among millions who currently use Western European languages (which all share the Latin script[13]), but it is a common phenomenon in those regions where multiple scripts exist, as with people among the Caucus Mountains (where people have used Cyrillic, Georgian, Armenian, Greek, Latin and Arabic scripts) and Southeast Asia (where there are scripts associated with each state - Vietnamese, Cambodian, Thai, Lao and Burmese). In fact, when the Albanians first began writing their language in the 19th century, the Ottoman Empire in which they lived already had many scripts, each associated with a language. This means the Albanian pioneers sought to create a unique alphabet despite all of those available to them in order to demonstrate the authenticity of their language[14]. While the Southeast of the United States is not an area with a large number of scripts, the Cherokee soon recognized the power that the distinctiveness of their writing had to differentiate Cherokee from non-Cherokee at a glance and bolster Cherokee pride.

With his syllabary complete, Sequoyah began to move around the Cherokee communities in North Carolina, Tennessee, Georgia and Alabama to promote his script. Meeting Cherokee leaders, he demonstrated the syllabary's effectiveness by writing down their words and having others not in the room (often his daughter) read them back, or by carrying personal messages between leaders in different communities. During this time, there was a growing number of educational institutions established for Cherokee and other native children, often by missionaries, so Sequoyah was eventually contracted to instruct boys at the Baptist Choctaw Academy in Georgetown, Kentucky. One of his students, a Cherokee Baptist minister, translated the New Testament into Cherokee using the syllabary and other Christian works - including hymns and other Biblical passages - were soon to follow.[15]

Impressed by the effectiveness of the script and its obvious popularity with an ever-growing number of students, the Cherokee Nation's government adopted the script as their official form of writing in 1825 and gave their blessing to education in it throughout all of the Cherokee communities. Two of Sequoyah's students were tasked with transcribing the Cherokee laws and

---

13 The one exception to this is Irish, which has its own script, which has faded in recent centuries. Interestingly, today it is only used by militant language enthusiasts and for symbolic uses like logos, official seals and bilingual signs, much in the same way that the Cherokee Syllabary is (as detailed in the last chapter).

14 "The Stamboul Alphabet of Shemseddin Sami Bey: Precursor to Turkish Script Reform" by Frances Trix (1999). In the *International Journal of Middle East Studies* V 31. Pgs 255 - 272

15 "Carvings from Cherokee Script's Dawn" by John Noble Wilford in the *New York Times* accessed online at: http://www.nytimes.com/2009/06/23/science/23cherokee.html?ref=science&_r=0

printing off multiple copies and distributing them throughout the Nation.[16]

A crucial turning point, perhaps even more important than the official adoption in 1826, came in 1828 when the first issue of the *Cherokee Phoenix* was printed. Published at the capital of the Cherokee in New Echota, Georgia, the *Phoenix* was the official newspaper of the Cherokee Nation and the first such document produced by any Native American group. The *Phoenix* was printed in the Cherokee language using both the syllabary and the English alphabet and included news (especially coverage of debates about Cherokee removal by the federal government), official statements of the Cherokee Nation, and opinion articles. While the *Phoenix* was a victim of the eventual removal of the Cherokee people and ceased publication on May 31, 1834, it was a seminal moment in promoting the syllabary and also in creating a sense of national identity and pride amongst the Cherokee[17].

The Cherokee Nation recognized the genius they had among them and created a special award for Sequoyah in 1824 that consisted of a silver medal in his honor and a "literary pension" so that he could write and work without worrying about his livelihood.[18] After that, he lived in Arkansas and served as a teacher and diplomat before traveling to Washington in 1828 to join in the negotiations regarding the new Indian Territory. After his return in 1829, he moved to the Indian Territory (today's Oklahoma) and re-established his home there. The home is now called Sequoyah's Cabin and remains a national historic site.[19]

16 "Invention of a New Alphabet" by Elias Boudinot (1832). *American Annals of Education.* V 4 No 1
17 "Cherokee Phoenix" in the *Encyclopedia of Oklahoma History and Culture* accessed online at:
    http://digital.library.okstate.edu/encyclopedia/entries/C/CH022.html
18 "About Sequoyah" at the homepage of the Sequoyah Museum online. Accessed online at:
    http://www.sequoyahmuseum.org/index.cfm/m/1/fuseAction/contentpage.main/detailID/29
19 "National Register of Historic Places Inventory Nomination: Sequoyah's Cabin" by the National Park Service.
    Accessed online at: http://pdfhost.focus.nps.gov/docs/NHLS/Text/66000634.pdf

Tonya Stinson's picture of Sequoyah's cabin

By now, Sequoyah was a major political figure within the nation and was traveling extensively during the debates about "removal" from the east (in particular Georgia) to the west (specifically the Indian Territory). Sequoyah advocated "reunification," which meant the eastern Cherokee joining their western brethren, and as a part of this mission, Sequoyah left the United States' territory in 1842 with a party of Cherokee to look for communities of their fellow members who had fled south of the border into Mexico to establish free communities. Sequoyah hoped to convince them to return, but he died on this journey - perhaps in 1843 or 1844 - and his body was buried by his companions in a location that has never been definitively identified.[20]

Chapter 5: Sequoyah's Syllabary and the "New Cherokee"

The Cherokee of the early 19th century were one of the so-called "Five Civilized Tribes," along with the Muscogee (Creek), Choctaw, Chickasaw and Seminole. These groups were located within what is now the Southeast United States, and the Muscogee and Cherokee lived in adjacent territories along the spine of the Appalachian Mountains in today's Northwest Georgia, Northeast Alabama, and southwest North Carolina.

It is important to note that the term "Civilized Tribe" is considered by many modern

---

20 "Sequoyah" at *Encyclopedia Britannica* online at:
http://www.britannica.com/EBchecked/topic/535250/Sequoyah

indigenous people as an insult, as it denies the status of "civilization" to any other groups in North American history and implies that "civilization" is only a product of contact with Europeans and attempts to assimilate. Scholarship has shown this to be categorically false, as pre-Columbian North America was home to numerous socially and technologically sophisticated groups, and even the smaller, more technologically simple groups had developed elaborate ethical and religious systems. While this term is not factually correct, it was commonly used at that time and did denote that there was something different about these five nations.

Under the Washington and Jefferson governments, intense efforts were made by the Federal Indian Agents to promote "civilization" and assimilation amongst the Native peoples across the territory of the new nation. This involved attempting to create a model of American society amongst these groups, including converting them, having them live in American-style homes, working private farms, promoting governmental institutions that mimicked American ones, and creating similar law codes. Amongst all of the Five Nations, the Cherokee themselves adopted the "civilized" status most strongly. By 1827, they had created a centralized government, with an independent supreme court and a written constitution. Many dressed like whites, converted to Christianity, and even held slaves, managing Southern-style plantations[21].

However, despite the beliefs of many sympathetic Americans who believed that the Cherokee desired to "become" white, the Cherokee adopted American ways as a defensive tactic. Realizing their increasingly helpless state against the U.S. military, they sought to become allies of the federal government in order to bolster their position against incursions by whites and the government of Georgia. In truth, the Cherokee way of life was not as far from "civilization" as many Europeans believed either, given that they had practiced intensive agriculture, lived in centralized settlements, and possessed elaborate forms of government for centuries before the Europeans' arrival[22].

Given this context, Sequoyah's syllabary came at the right time and the right place for the Cherokee. The Cherokee at the time sought to achieve a difficult balance between assimilation into white society and the maintenance of their own distinct identity. The Cherokee Nation government also sought to bolster its own legitimacy as it became increasingly similar to white models and more distant from traditional modes of governance among the Cherokee. Undoubtedly, the continued widespread use of the Cherokee language was seen as one of the primary bolsters of this identity; as long as the Cherokee spoke Cherokee, their identity could be seen as safe.

Needless to say, Sequoyah's syllabary seemed a perfect fit for this circumstance. It was uniquely Cherokee and inextricably tied to the Cherokee language, and it was also thoroughly

21 "Five Civilized Tribes" in the *Encyclopedia of Oklahoma History and Culture* accessed online at: http://digital.library.okstate.edu/encyclopedia/entries/F/FI011.html
22 *1491: New Revelations of the Americas Before Columbus* by Charles C. Mann (2006). Vintage Books.

"modern" and "civilized" and allowed the Cherokee Government to pursue white activities like constitution-writing while arguing that they did not betray their past. It was also a tool for showing whites (and possibly other Native peoples) that the "new" Cherokee were not simply mimics of their white neighbors but in fact creating their own, equal society in parallel to American society. The fact that the Cherokee Nation could effectively control the syllabary by controlling the printing presses in the script (the *Cherokee Phoenix* was owned by the Nation) and the schools meant that it did not present any threat to the government's legitimacy.

All of those reasons bolstered the use of the syllabary, but they do not fully account for the rapid manner in which everyday Cherokees adopted the Syllabary. The system's popularity with the Cherokee was due not only to its suitability to the language (nobody learns to read simply because a writing system is well-designed) but also to the fact it was also a system that was a good fit for the increasingly fractured nature of Cherokee life. During the early 19th century, the Cherokee people were being continually pushed out of their lands, and occasionally they were being pushed out of lands that they had been pushed into only a few years earlier. This meant that previously stable communities and relationships that could rely upon regular visits (such as family relationships) or emissaries (such as between political leaders and allies) were increasingly difficult to maintain, because the individuals involved were becoming scattered across the Southeast, from Georgia and the Carolinas in the east all the way to Texas and Oklahoma in the west. The syllabary gave the Cherokee the ability to maintain a sense of themselves as a community, as a people, and to keep up their vitally important relationships with one another.

The Cherokee were not alone in the importance that writing played in forging their identity as a people. In his famous book *Imagined Communities*, Benedict Anderson writes that the printed word, written in vernacular languages (languages that were not the Greek and Latin versions of scholarly works) served as the most important vehicle for developing a sense of national identity amongst the peoples of Europe, including the Germans, French, and Italians. While the sacred language, Latin, evoked in its readers a sense of pan-Christian solidarity and the idea that a community could theoretically extend out someday to all of humanity, writing in the vernacular language involved communication with a far more finite group: one's fellow language-speakers. Moreover, for the first time, an author could feel that he or she could speak directly to this finite yet very large community through the printed word. Anderson called them "imagined" communities, since even the smallest European language included far more people than any single individual could meet over the course of his or her lifespan, which meant that any connection to those people must be at least partly imagined. This type of cultural and political solidarity was new in human history and led to people developing a new sense of self in the process[23].

---

23 *Imagined Communities: Reflections on the Origin and Spread of Nationalism* by Benedict Anderson (1983). Verso Books.

Sequoyah wanted to give his people what he saw as the one great technological tool the Europeans and Americans had, and one that gave them great military and administrative advantages at that. In one sense, he was wrong, because while writing helped whites spread across the continent and subdue Native Americans, it was ultimately disease and inter-native conflict that brought down the Cherokee and other groups. On the other hand, Sequoyah could not have been more correct, because by creating his writing system Sequoyah gave his people a powerful tool for recreating their communities in the new era, for maintaining their sense of self, and for creating a new, imagined community around the shared written word. More than any other single Cherokee in history, Sequoyah helped establish the modern Cherokee Nation, one of the largest Native American political units today[24], and one that managed to survive the horrors of the Trail of Tears and generations of brutal oppression at that.

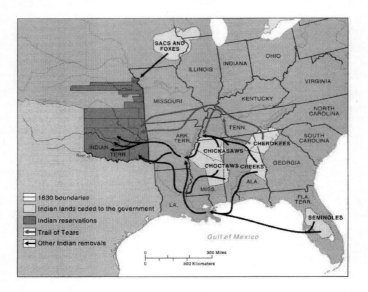

The forced removal of Native Americans in the Southeast

---

24 More individuals claim to be Cherokee in the US census than any other native group. However, the Cherokee Nation believes that many of these claims are spurious and that the number of authentic, registered Cherokees is much lower. The state that according to their numbers, the Navajo are the largest native group today while the Cherokee are the second-largest.

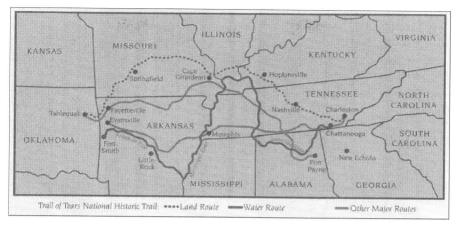

The Cherokee's routes during the Trail of Tears

Chapter 6: Understanding the Syllabary

R D W Ir G Ꮽ Ꮿ P ᴧ Ꮣ Ꭹ Ꮺ Ь P Ꮈ M
ᏓᎵ Ꮿ ᏺ W B Ꮱ Ꮛ Ꮬ Ꮧ G Ꮁ A Ꮷ Ꮿ 4
ᏆᎨ C Ꮖ Ꮽ H Ꮤ Z Ꮎ Ꮳ R Ꮀ S V Ꮅ Ꮑ
E Ꮎ T Ꮳ Ꮰ Ꮱ Ꮝ J K Ꮴ Ꮱ Θ Ꮐ Ꮆ Ꮹ
Ꮷ Ꮯ S Ꮥ Ꮐ i Ꮳ Ꮏ Ꮝ Ꮆ Ꮲ Ꭾ Ꮅ H
Ꮅ Ꮓ Ꮐ Ꮸ L Ꮏ Ꮯ Ꮽ Ꮚ &

This is a picture of the syllabary in the way Sequoyah originally ordered it. "G" is marked in red to indicate it is no longer used.

One of the most common misconceptions about Sequoyah is that he was the inventor of the Cherokee alphabet, an understandable mistake given that for modern users of English, the ideas of a written script and an alphabet are one and the same. Perhaps, if pushed, many might recognize that Chinese characters are not connected to sounds in the way that an alphabet is but instead to concepts. However, familiarity with an alphabet makes it hard to understand exactly what the difference is, much less how to name it.

What Sequoyah created was a syllabary, a system of writing where each character (a character is the generic term for a single unit of writing, so in alphabets they are typically called "letters") refs not to a single sound but to a discrete syllable. In other words, if English were written syllabically, it would not have a letter "b" but instead a symbol for "be," "ba," "bo," "boo," and "bi," which represent all the different ways the letter "b" is used in pronunciation. Syllabaries tend to have more available characters than alphabets, but far fewer than "logographic" writing systems like Chinese that have characters for concepts. A syllabary has the advantage over alphabetic systems of better capturing written sounds without confusion and for using fewer characters to write a word. For example, the English version of Sequoyah's name that is the closest to the spoken Cherokee name is "Ssiquoya", which has eight characters. Those same three syllables, "ssi - quo - ya" are written in Sequoyah's own script with only three characters: ☐☐☐. This means that a syllabary is a bit more difficult to learn than an alphabet because it has more characters, but at the same time, it is more efficient to write.

While syllabaries are not common in the European languages (all of the modern European scripts - Latin, Cyrillic and Greek - are alphabets, not syllabaries), they have been independently created numerous times in human history. In addition to the Cherokee language, other Native American languages to later have syllabaries include Cree, Inuktitut, Ojibwe, Blackfoot, and Naskapi. The most commonly used examples, however, come from across the Pacific, most notably the Hiragana and Katakana syllabaries (often erroneously referred to as "alphabets") of Japan and the Eskayan syllabary of the Philippines. Abandoned syllabaries were used in Europe (Cypriot, Iberian and Celtiberian), Africa (Vai, Mende, Loma, Kpelle, Bamum and Ndjuka) and even amongst small groups in China (the Yi script and the Nushu women's script made famous in the book *Snow Flower and the Secret Fan* are examples)[25]. While it is difficult to say without any doubts, current scholarship holds that the Linear B writing system of Mycenaean Greek (previously untranslatable) is in fact a syllabary, not an alphabet, meaning that this form of writing was present amongst the earliest literate peoples of Europe.

Given that there are numerous other syllabaries, how does the Cherokee system compare and contrast with others?[26] To begin with, the size of the syllabary (85 standard characters), while much larger than the 26 letter English alphabet, is not remarkable in itself. The Plains Cree syllabary has 70 main symbols plus nine ending symbols, the Inuktitut syllabary has 105 symbols, and the Japanese Hiragana syllabary has 46 basic symbols, 5 long vowel symbols and 61 additional sound symbols.

What does differentiate the Cherokee system from these others is in its aesthetics. An individual examining other syllabaries without the ability to read them is often struck by the harmoniousness of their characters. For example, the Cree syllabary, which was created by a Methodist missionary in the 1840s, is constructed largely of right triangles facing in different directions and accompanied by between zero and three dots. Other symbols appear to be akin to

25 "Syllabaries" at the *Omniglot* website. Accessed online at: http://www.omniglot.com/writing/syllabaries.htm
26 "Cherokee Syllabary" at the *Omniglot* website. Accessed online at:
http://www.omniglot.com/writing/cherokee.htm

the lower-case English "b", or an "L" or a "J" or a squiggle with sharp or rounded edges, each oriented in different directions and potentially accompanied by a dot. The simplicity of the lines, the crispness of the small angles, and the widespread use of the dots gives a remarkable harmoniousness to the writing[27]. While very different in its appearance, Japanese Hiragana is similarly harmonious in its forms. The characters are all written in a swooping style made up of many individual brush strokes, which gives it a handwritten, calligraphic appearance similar to many East Asian scripts, but Hiragana is distinct for its looseness and lightness of style and the simplicity of the characters. Since it is often used in very small characters written above a main text in another Japanese script (they have three) in order to clarify a term, the Hiragana characters must be very simple or their details would be obscured[28].

The Cherokee syllabary, on the other hand, demonstrates neither simplicity in its characters nor harmoniousness across the entire system. If anything, the characters appear to be something of a grab-bag, with many drawn directly from Latin (English) script or Arabic numerals. Furthermore, since the syllabary does not have case, both upper-case and lower-case Latin letters are used as individual Cherokee characters. Others appear to have been begun as Latin letters but then have curlicues and flourishes added to differentiate them. Many of these differences took the form of serifs, which is a small line attached to the end of a stroke of the pen used to make a character. Modern Latin fonts are divided between the Serif, such as Times New Roman, and the Non-Serif or Sans-Serif, such as Arial. There is considerable debate about whether legibility is improved or harmed by serifs in Latin script, but in the Cherokee syllabary, they are absolutely necessary.

There also may have been practical reasons for this. In Sequoyah's day, the most important technology for the written word was the printing press, which was loaded with individual letters made up of small square metal pieces called type. It was expensive to have distinctive Cherokee type created in large enough numbers to print texts like a newspaper, so the price of printing would have been kept within a reasonable level by using already-available Latin type or by creating characters which could be created by buying Latin type and then modifying the pieces individually by hand. The early Albanian and Turkish alphabetic experimenters discovered something similar; they could buy the letter "i" and simply file off the dot on top of the letter to create a new symbol: "ı". At least at the scripts' starts, this could keep costs within reason.

In Sequoya's case, the overall effect is to create a syllabary which, when written, has a baroque beauty to it. It has a feeling of complexity, difficulty and sophistication, though it can also be interpreted as being overly-complicated, difficult to write, and intimidating. Sequoyah, completely isolated from debates (which mostly occurred long after his death) about the

---

27 "Inuktitut Syllabary" at the *Omniglot* website. Accessed online at:
   http://www.omniglot.com/writing/inuktitut.htm
28 "Japanese Hirgana" at the *Omniglot* website. Accessed online at:
   http://www.omniglot.com/writing/japanese_hiragana.htm

importance of simplicity for comprehension of script, created a form of writing which may be unnecessarily complicated, but it nevertheless possesses a strange beauty of its own.

a			e	i	o	u	v [ə̃]
D a			R e	T i	Ꭳ o	Ꝋ u	i v
Ꭶ ga	Ꭰ ka		Ꝉ ge	Ꭹ gi	A go	J gu	E gv
Ꭷ ha			Ꮲ he	Ꭿ hi	Ꝉ ho	Ꮁ hu	Ꭽ hv
W la			Ꮥ le	P li	G lo	M lu	Ꮕ lv
Ꮿ ma			Ꭺ me	H mi	Ꮵ mo	Ꮿ mu	
Θ na	Ꮏ hna	G nah	Ꮑ ne	h ni	Z no	Ꮔ nu	Ꝋ nv
Ꭲ qua			Ꮳ que	Ꮖ qui	Ꝟ quo	Ꝏ quu	Ɛ quv
Ꮪ s	Ꮁ sa		4 se	b si	Ꝉ so	Ꮙ su	R sv
Ꮣ da	W ta		Ꮥ de	Ꮒ te	Ꮠ di	Ꮱ ti	A do	S du	Ꝺ dv
Ꮸ dla	Ꮳ tla		L tle	C tli	Ꮿ tlo	Ꮿ tlu	P tlv
G tsa			Ꮴ tse	Ꮳ tsi	K tso	Ꮷ tsu	C tsv
Ꮐ wa			Ꮾ we	Θ wi	Ꮼ wo	9 wu	6 wv
Ꮿ ya			ꞵ ye	Ꭹ yi	ꞙ yo	G yu	B yv

A picture of the syllabary's characters and their corresponding English syllables

Chapter 7: The Cherokee Language

The syllabary is used on this stop sign in Tahlequah, Oklahoma

The Cherokee language was (and continues to be) one of the largest indigenous languages of North America, and the Cherokee name for it is written in English as either "Tsalagi" or "Tslagi." It is written in the Syllabary as "☐☐☐". The origins of the name "Cherokee" is a bit obscure, but it was apparently adopted from one of their enemies, and today, most Cherokee (including the Cherokee Nation Government) have adopted the English name.

Today, the Cherokee language is still spoken by roughly 10,400 individuals divided into several groups: roughly a thousand still in North Carolina, with most of the remainder in Arkansas and Oklahoma. This is roughly 8.5% of the 122,000 individuals registered with the Cherokee nation, and there are only about 100 individuals for whom Cherokee is their only language. In addition to use within Cherokee families, the language is also taught in Cherokee schools and at the University of Oklahoma and Northeast Oklahoma University. Somewhere between 15% and 20% can read it, and 5% can write in the language.[29]

Compared to most indigenous languages, these are very impressive numbers, showing a language with ongoing vitatlity and possibility for real community participation. However, it is a mere shadow of the strength that the language knew in Sequoyah's time. Not only did almost all of the Cherokee speak the language fluently, many were monolingual, and it was the principal language of daily life for many communities. In fact, Sequoyah's syllabary was so enthusiastically adopted that the Cherokee quickly developed literacy levels above those of surrounding white communities, and there was a vibrant audience for religious, government and other types of publications.

In his masterful analysis of the deciphering of the Maya written language, Michael Coe examined all of the various forms of script found in human history. His discussion of why syllabaries are suitable to some languages and not other is an excellent starting point for an analysis of the suitability of Cherokee: "Some languages are amenable to such visual treatment [as a syllabary], some less so, and some not at all. At the upper end of the amenability scale is Japanese, with its predominantly [consonant-vowel] syllabic structure (*sa-shi-mi*, *Yo-ko-ha-ma*), and such a script was devised by the Japanese back in our Dark Ages. At the other end are languages like our own with dense consonant clusters. For instance, the city of Scranton in Pennsylvania might have to be written syllabically as *Su-cu-ra-na-to-n(o)* with the final *o* suppressed in speaking."[30]

Like Japanese, Cherokee is just such a syllabic language; in fact, when it is written out in Latin characters, syllables are often divided by hyphens, at least in those texts prepared for learners. As such, the syllabary was not only a significant symbolic victory for the Cherokee seeking to

29 "Cherokee: A Language of the United States" at the *Ethnologue* website. Accessed online at: http://www.ethnologue.com/language/chr
30 *Breaking the Maya Code* by Michael D. Coe (1999). Thames and Hudson Books. Quote on pg 28.

promote their ethnic identity and political autonomy but also a technical triumph because it was a form of writing that is excellently suited to its form of speaking.

Despite this suitability, use of the syllabary suffered during the mid-19th century. The first major setback to the language came about with the Trail of Tears, when tens of thousands of indigenous people were forcibly removed from the Southeast (especially Georgia) to make way for white farmers and miners and were resettled in Oklahoma, the "Indian Territory." The move had a terrible human cost in lives lost (somewhere between 2,000-6,000 Cherokee died along the way), but it also took a linguistic toll as well. The printing presses that used the syllabary (especially the offices of the *Cherokee Phoenix* newspaper) were largely based in Georgia and never reopened. Furthermore, as the Cherokee left behind their schools, churches, offices, printing presses, and libraries and were forced to completely restart their communities, basic survival took precedence over literary affairs in the new reservation life for at least the first generation.

While use of the syllabary suffered during this period, the language itself continued to be the primary means of communication in Cherokee communities, which always left open the possibility of a revival in the use of the Syllabary. This revival became much harder in the 20th century, especially in the 1950s, when the Cherokee youth were forcibly removed en-masse from their home communities and sent to mult-ethnic boarding schools with children from other indigenous nations. The goal was assimilation, and the children were forced to abandon the use of Cherokee and adopt American language and habits. In the process, the community dropped from 75% bilingual to 5% bilingual in a single generation, and the forced assimilation attempts are responsible for the fact that only 10% of the Cherokee are now bilingual. It's actually impressive that there has been a doubling of the percentage of the population since the 1950s[31]. Nonetheless, among those who are literate, today's speakers are just as likely to use the Latin characters taught in the boarding schools as the Cherokee syllabary.

Chapter 8: Sequoyah's Modern Legacy

More than perhaps any other Native American, Sequoyah has been almost universally respected by Native Americans and whites alike. The number of honors given to him in his life and after are remarkable. Among countless examples, the great Sequoia trees of California bear his name, there was a proposal to found a "State of Sequoyah" in today's Eastern and Southern Oklahoma in the early 20th century[32], he lived in what became Sequoyah County in Oklahoma, there is a Sequoyah Research Center for indigenous writing in Arkansas, a Mount Sequoyah on the Tennessee-North Carolina border, the Sequoyah Hills outside of Knoxville Tennessee, and numerous other places and things bearing his name. These include the former U.S. presidential

---

31 "Native Languages of the Americas: Cherokee (Tsalagi)" at the *Index of American Indian Languages.* Accessed online at: http://www.native-languages.org/cherokee.htm
32 "The State of Sequoyah" in *The New York Times* 5 October, 1905. Accessed online at: http://query.nytimes.com/mem/archive-free/pdf?res=9E01EED7113BE631A25756C0A9669D946497D6CF

yacht, a North Carolina golf course, a nuclear plant in Tennessee, and many high schools and elementary schools. All of these honors go to show the uniqueness of his accomplishment in American history.

When Sequoyah's name is mentioned, a point is often brought up that he was the only person in history who was illiterate but still managed to create a writing system for his native tongue out of whole cloth. This statement has been repeated so often that its authenticity is taken for granted, but while it may have been true in Sequoyah's day, it is definitely not today. In 1959, a peasant farmer from Laos named Shong Lue Yang claimed to have experienced a series of visions in which he encountered a pair of divine male twins who taught him how to use a sacred script. Yang was a member of a marginalized ethnic group called the Hmong; living in the Lao Highlands, the Hmong had long been aware of writing among the Laotian and Vietnamese lowlanders but had never adopted it for themselves. Throughout the 1960s, as the Vietnam War raged around him and his people, Shong Lue Yang ("The Mother of Writing" among his people) taught literacy and created a system of educational institutions. Eventually, he was executed in 1971 by supporters of the Royal Lao Government in the Lao Civil War[33].

Shong Lue Yang

Like Sequoyah, Shong Lue Yang was illiterate and a member of a marginalized indigenous group in a world torn by war and the dispossession of his people's lands. Unlike Sequoyah, Yang positioned himself as a religious messiah and considered his script a divine gift, which made him an opponent of the government. Conversely, Sequoyah was more than willing to put his new script to the Cherokee Nation's use from the beginning. In both societies, the function of

33 *Mother of Writing: The Origin and Development of a Hmong Messianic Script* by William Allen Smalley and Chia Koua Vang (1990). University of Chicago Press.

writing was well understood, even if the technical details were not; while Yang saw his script as divinely inspired, he also saw it (like Sequoyah did) as eminently practical. In Yang's case, he created different versions for sacred and secular activities.

Some might be disappointed to hear that Sequoyah is not unique in his accomplishment, but the truth is there were probably others who created whole scripts from scratch without the ability to read even before him. Nonetheless, the fact that at least one other individual matched his feat does not detract from the difficulty that Sequoyah faced, nor does it cheapen the beauty and functionality of his creation.

In 1971, the scholarship and discussion of Sequoyah was deeply shaken by the publication of the book *Tell Them The Lie: The Sequoyah Myth*, which was authored by a Cherokee man named Traveller Bird who claimed to be a direct descendant of the man in question. Traveller Bird asserted that most of what was "known" about Sequoyah was in fact a distortion of the truth created by white historians who could not erase the man but instead sought to twist his story to their advantage. Traveller Bird claimed that instead of being a half-Cherokee, half-white man who invented a syllabary based upon observations of European writing systems, Sequoyah was a pure-blood Cherokee who was the last of a clan of scribes who had passed down a secrete syllabic writing system since the pre-Columbian era.

The book was popular enough to warrant attention,[34] but there is no evidence to support his claim beyond the assertion that he learned this information through the stories of his family. It is one thing to invent a writing system without being able to read, but it has always been presumed that Sequoyah was aware of the concept of writing due to his contacts with whites. To not be aware of the concept of writing and actually invent writing itself is even more difficult; in fact, it is only known to have occurred three times in human history,[35] and it is always a multi-century project which leaves behind many traces. Could the Cherokee scribe's clan have truly eliminated all writing from pots, clothing, texts, funerary rituals, and other artifacts from the entire continent of North America? It is simply absurd to think that such a process could be hidden. Furthermore, while the syllabary is quite obviously a work of unique genius, it is also quite obviously derived in its forms from Latin script. Each of the three times that writing was invented in human history, the form of the script was so unique that it could never be mistaken for one of the other types of writing (for instance, no one would mistake Chinese characters for Mayan glyphs or Irish letters).

Traveller Bird's writing was part of a larger context of cultural reclamation and pride amongst

---

34 "Sequoya ca 1770, ca 1840" in the *New Georgia Encyclopedia* by Ted Wadley (2002). Accessed online at: http://www.georgiaencyclopedia.org/articles/history-archaeology/sequoyah-ca-1770-ca-1840

35 Once was in China - a tradition that led to the logographic systems of Chinese, Japanese and others today. Another was in Mesopotamia, which led to all of the other modern writing systems, from Arabic to the Cherokee Syllabary. The third was in Mesoamerica, which led to Mayan, Zapotec and Aztec writing, but was a tradition which was snuffed out by European colonialism.

Native Americans at the time. This was marked by the major events of the history of the American Indian Movement (AIM), such as the 1968 founding of the group, the 1969-1971 occupation of Alcatraz Island in the San Francisco Bay, the 1972 March on Washington, and leading up to the 1973 standoff at Wounded Knee[36]. These events radicalized an entire generation of young Native Americans who sought to decolonize their cultures and recapture their former dignity and strength. Much of this was tremendously positive, but unfortunately, it also led to a lionization of racial thinking, obsession with blood purity, and a rejection of any native cultural elements believed to be product of assimilation into white society. The Cherokee have not been immune to this thinking, and the ongoing controversy of whether to expel the descendants of former Cherokee slaves (the "Cherokee Freedmen") is an expression of this purist, racial belief system[37]. Traveller Bird's book is firmly within this trend and must be treated with the same suspicion and disappointment as arguments for racial purity in any other group.

While Traveller Bird attempted to fundamentally alter the Sequoyah story, he interestingly did not try to completely oust the place of the man in Cherokee history. This may be because Sequoyah stands head and shoulders above other Cherokee figures in the imagination of not only Cherokee but many other citizens of the United States. Sequoyah has taken his place in the pantheon of early citizens of the United States, and among the Cherokee, he fills a role of a vitally important "founding father" of the modern Cherokee nation.

One place where his life is commemorated is at the Sequoyah's Birthplace Museum. Located alongside the Fort Loudon State Historic Site and nestled on the northern boundary of the Great Smoky Mountains National Park, the site is owned by the Eastern Band of Cherokee Indians, a group which violently resisted the westward relocation of the Trail of Tears along with their leader Tsali. Living nearby in a region called the Qualla Boundary, today they are caretakers of many of the sites historically associated with the Cherokee people, including the museum. The Eastern Band has also used the Cherokee Syllabary in its capital, the town of Cherokee, North Carolina, where all of the road signs are bilingual.[38]

---

36 "American Indian Movement" at the *Encyclopedia Britannica* online at:
   http://www.britannica.com/EBchecked/topic/19799/American-Indian-Movement
37 "A Race or a Nation? Cherokee National Identity and the Status of Freedmen's Descendents" by Alan Ray
   (2007) in the *Michigan Journal of Race and Law* vo. 12
38 The homepage of the *Sequoyah Birthplace Museum* accessed online at: http://www.sequoyahmuseum.org/

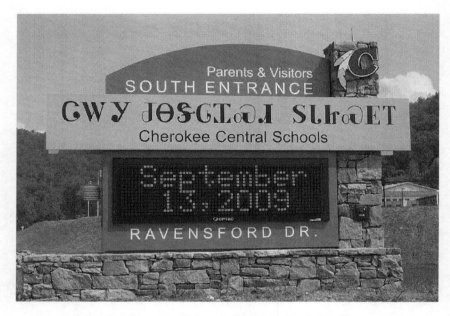

A sign using the syllabary in Cherokee, North Carolina

At the same time, the Cherokee are a large group - there are hundreds of thousands of them under three autonomous tribal governments - and not all of them agree on anything, even the importance of Sequoyah and the Cherokee syllabary. One of the main problems with the syllabary is the fact that it is difficult to differentiate between the various characters, many of which differ only in the additions of small curves or serifs on them. Thus, they can be confusing when read from a distance, when written by hand, or in general for new learners. This means that while open criticism is often muted by national pride, the Cherokee today have largely abandoned the syllabary when writing their language in all but formal situations.[39]

Criticisms aside, people do continue to use the syllabary today, despite many setbacks for the language. It is difficult to say how many people actually write to one another using the syllabary, or who use it for everyday tasks like making shopping lists or reminding their children they have band practice, but it is safe to guess that among more militant language-learners and users, there are probably a few who do attempt to use the syllabary for all basic tasks, regardless of its potential difficulties.

---

39 "The Mystery of Why the Cherokee Syllabary Sucks" Apr 8, 2011. Accessed online at:
   http://sheikhjahbooty.wordpress.com/2011/04/08/the-mystery-of-why-the-cherokee-syllabary-sucks/

Generally speaking, however, the syllabary is primarily used today as a symbolic marker of "Cherokee-ness." Words in the syllabary appear in places like the official flag and seals of all three modern Cherokee tribal governments, as well as in official events and documents, on bilingual road signs in Cherokee-controlled towns, and on the logos of Cherokee organizations. The ubiquity of these uses, as well as their essentially unnecessary nature (since they are always accompanied with English) means that they are a way that non-Cherokee speaking members of the community can feel a pride and connection to the language.

That said, not all of modern uses of the syllabary have been nostalgic or historically-minded. For instance, the release of Windows 8 from Microsoft was fully compatible with both the syllabary, and the language and a large number of new computer words have been coined. For example, those who use the syllabary can write □□□□ for "keyboard," □□□ for "subfolders," □□□□□ for "spellcheck," and □□□□□ for "paste."[40] Similarly, the Cherokee Nation (as well as a number of independent language enthusiasts) have created numerous fonts for using the language on the computer.[41] The flexibility of computer fonts to make any character shape may actually allow more people to use the syllabary than before. Furthermore, there is also interest in alternative hand-written forms of the syllabary that Sequoyah developed but abandoned during his lifetime, if only because some language users find them to be more fluid and easier to use[42]. In the last few decades, the *Cherokee Phoenix* has been revived by the Cherokee Nation, and on its electronic edition, it always includes at least one article using the syllabary[43].

As all of this makes clear, from its inception, the syllabary has been closely tied to the Cherokee's national identity. The syllabary was also a handmaiden of the Cherokee Nation, accompanying the new government as it consolidated itself, and it aided the Cherokee people in their transformation into a modern ethnicity with a sense of themselves as a nation of people connected to each other through the written word. While it has not fulfilled Sequoyah's original goal of setting his people on an equal political and military footing with whites, nor his later goal of serving as a means of regular everyday communication between Cherokees, the syllabary still serves several important purposes. It is a marker of a unique identity, a source of pride, and a piece of powerful heritage which still serves as a unifier of Cherokee identity across the people's many homelands, governments and religious and social organizations.

Bibliography

Bender, Margaret. (2002) Signs of Cherokee Culture: Sequoyah's Syllabary in Eastern Cherokee Life. Chapel Hill: University of North Carolina Press.

---

40 "Cherokee Computer -- □ □ □ □□□□□□□ □□□□□□□□" at the Tsasuyed Blog. Accessed online at: http://tsasuyed.blogspot.com/
41 The Cherokee Nation's official font can be downloaded at: http://www.cherokee.org/AboutTheNation/Language/CherokeeFont.aspx
42 An example would be at the *Ani Kutani* Website, accessed online at: http://www.ani-kutani.com/ (warning: Cherokee Language site)
43 *Cherokee Phoenix* Homepage. Accessed online at: http://www.cherokeephoenix.org/

Feeling, Durbin. Cherokee-English Dictionary: Tsalagi-Yonega Didehlogwasdohdi. Tahlequah, Oklahoma: Cherokee Nation, 1975: xvii

Holmes, Ruth Bradley; Betty Sharp Smith (1976). Beginning Cherokee: Talisgo Galiquogi Dideliquasdodi Tsalagi Digoweli. Norman: University of Oklahoma Press. ISBN 0-8061-1362-6.

Foreman, Grant, Sequoyah, University of Oklahoma Press, Norman, OK, 1938.

Langguth, A. J. Driven West: Andrew Jackson and the Trail of Tears to the Civil War. New York, Simon & Schuster. 2010. ISBN 978-1-4165-4859-1.

McKinney, Thomas and Hall, James, History of the Indian Tribes of North America. (Philadelphia, PA, 1837–1844).

McLoughlin, William G., After the Trail of Tears: The Cherokees' Struggle for Sovereignty 1839 - 1880. University of North Carolina Press. Chapel Hill. 1993

Made in the USA
Coppell, TX
19 August 2021